King of the Cowboys

ROY ROGERS
King of the Cowboys

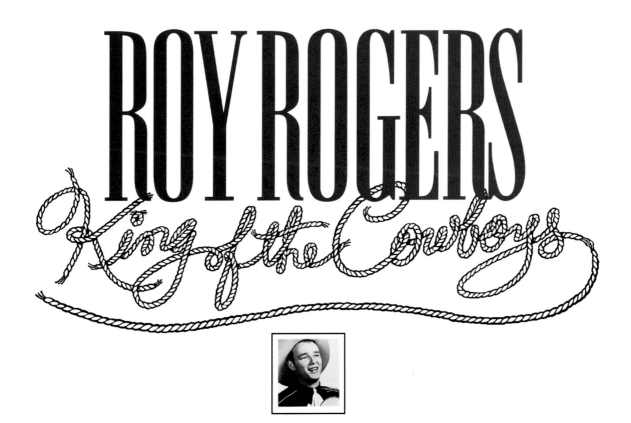

by
Georgia Morris
and **Mark Pollard**

CollinsPublishersSanFrancisco

A Division of HarperCollins*Publishers*

First published by Collins Publishers San Francisco
1160 Battery Street, San Francisco, California 94111

Copyright © 1994 Second Son Entertainment Company / Galen Films

All photographs courtesy of the Roy Rogers and Dale Evans Museum

Introduction by Georgia Morris
Designed by Mark Pollard
Cover designed by Mark Pollard/Steve Sikora

Library of Congress Cataloging-in-Publication Data

Rogers Roy, 1911-
Roy Rogers : king of the cowboys / [edited] by Georgia Morris and Mark Pollard
p. cm.
ISBN 0-00-255334-1
ISBN 0-00-255449-6 (limited ed.)
1. Rogers, Roy, 1911- . 2. Actors–United States–Biography.
3. Singers–United States–Biography.
I. Morris, Georgia, 1948- . II. Pollard, Mark (Mark Lawrence), 1956- .
III. Title. IV. Title: King of the cowboys.
PN2287. R73A3 1994
791.43'028'092–dc20
[B]   93-35483
CIP

Printed in Italy
1 2 3 4 5 6 7 8 9 0

Roy on location, UNDER WESTERN STARS, 1938.

INTRODUCTION

Roy Rogers hit the newsstands on the cover of Life Magazine, July 12, 1943. Rearing on his famous palomino Trigger, with the undeveloped San Fernando Valley at his feet, Roy was the stuff of American dreams . . . a movie star, cowboy hero with a future.

Born Leonard Franklin Slye on November 5, 1911, Roy started his ascent to King of the Cowboy status from boyhood beginnings on a home-made Ohio River houseboat, built by the sweat and dreams of his dad and blind uncle. From houseboat to farm life in the hills of Ohio, Roy's roots are at the heart of America and have steadied him through sixty years of entertaining and decades of mega-stardom.

Roy Rogers starred in 81 westerns for Republic Pictures. In 1947, over 900,000 fans wrote personal heartfelt letters to Roy. Of his 2000 fan clubs, London's chapter was the largest with 50,000 members. In the late '40's he beat out James Mason and Bing Crosby as England's most popular movie star. Republic Pictures smiled on their singing cowboy. In the states, eighty million movie tickets were sold in 1948. And then came television. Each week, Roy left the Double R Bar Ranch for adventures with Dale Evans in 100 films for TV. On any Saturday in 1957, kids turned off their sets when the Roy Rogers Show was over and ran to the newsstand for the current issue of the Dell comic book . . . two million kids per monthly issue. With 105,000 fans jamming the Los Angeles Coliseum, the Roy Rogers Rodeo set box office records around the world. It has been calculated that Roy smiled from the front of two and a half billion boxes of Post cereal! These are the statistics of an American icon.

The span of Roy's career embraces all the media of our time. When he founded the Sons of the Pioneers in 1934, a new and modern era of country music was about to unfold, leaving hillbilly music behind for the smoother sounds of "Cool Water" and "Tumbling Tumbleweeds." From a first recording on Decca Records on August 8th of that year, Roy has made hundreds of recordings over the years. His latest album, Tribute, released on RCA in 1991, drew the biggest stars in country music to sing with their cowboy hero.

A generation of kids and adults scrambled through Sunday dinner to tune in their radio sets at 6pm for Roy's country humor, music and adventure in Paradise Valley, brought to them on the Mutual Network by Quaker Oats. All the while recording, performing on radio and in public appearances, Roy remained King of the Cowboys at the box office from 1943 till he phased out his movies to television.

Roy Rogers and his wife, Dale Evans, the Queen of the west herself, managed to raise a multicultural family in the 1950's . . . not a time noted for its openness. The Rogers clan was an inspiration. They traveled on the road together when school was out, to keep a balance of work and family togetherness under the glare of the Hollywood spotlight. And, as always, Roy found time between shows at Madison Square Garden or Wembley Stadium in London to play to the forgotten kids in hospitals and orphanages everywhere.

There have been a lot of clean-cut celluloid cowboys, but what is it about Roy? In 1989, at the Annual Roy Rogers Festival in Portsmouth, Ohio, grown men wept as Roy and Dale sang "Happy Trails" for fans who had "waited all their lives for this." Songwriter Jim Bowman summed up Roy's effect on him in his lyrics . . .

What would the King of the Cowboys do
Standing in my boots?
Could he recognize the bad guys?
Would he fight or would he shoot?
It's hard to wear a white hat today,
and make it through.
But I've never been steered wrong yet
Wondering what ol' Roy would do.

We all feel that we know him and that, in the words of a childhood fan, "I believed then as I do now, that if Roy Rogers knew I needed him, he would come." What is it about Roy that makes people feel this way? Perhaps the answer is here in his own plain words. G.M.

Roy and Trigger, 1943.

The first picture Roy and I made together was THE COWBOY AND THE SENORITA. I was very impressed by Roy's down-to-earth personality, his zeal for his performances in front of a camera, his friendliness with his entire cast and crew—and most of all his love for children and elderly people. Aside from these attributes, one could not be around him without being charmed by the squint of his blue eyes and easy smile.

(above) Dale Evans in a Republic Pictures publicity photo.

Roy has been a wonderful husband, father and friend. We share our Christian faith. People ask, "How have you been able to stay together all these years?" To that I reply: "The Lord is the head of our home, we never let the sun go down on our wrath, nor let disagreements fester overnight."

To me, his wife, Roy Rogers is indeed "The King of the Cowboys," and richly deserves the title.

DALE EVANS ROGERS

THROUGH THIS DOOR PASS
ROY ROGERS
(AND HIS) HORSE TRIGGER
NOW PLAYING

Roy on tour, 1941.

(above) Roy age 20, on his bike, 1931.
(below left) Roy with his sisters, Christmas, 1932.
(below right) On the road, outside Lancaster, PA, 1941.
(opposite) Roy and first wife, Arlene, with their parents, (l to r) Prentice and Lucy Wilkins and Mattie and Andy Slye, 1939.

I'm just an old country boy from Duck Run, Ohio, who happened to get a job in the entertainment world.

I always felt the kids were a part of me, you know, because if it wasn't for those children, I wouldn't be here. If they didn't speak their piece and show you they liked you, there wouldn't be a **Roy Rogers**.

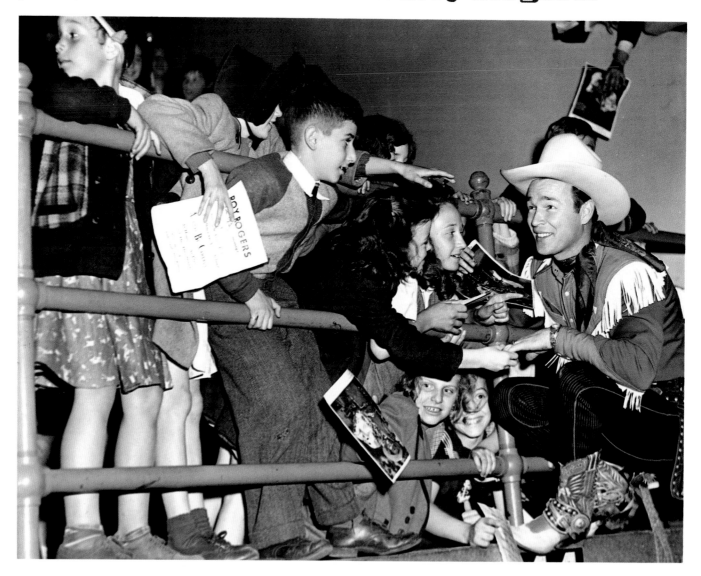

(opposite)
Autographing programs at a rodeo performance for underprivileged children.
(above) swamped by fans at the Miller Theater, Milwaukee, Wisconsin.
(below left) A smooch from fan Michael Meltzer, age 4, of Brooklyn, New York.
(below right) Reaching for Roy.

I just accepted the fans as part of my life, I
had to or I wouldn't be here. I knew what I was
going to run into, every trip, wherever I went.
But when you're in show business, you either
keep going or you don't. You can fold up and
end up as yesterday, you know what I mean?

(opposite) Young Roy, surrounded.
(above) Covering a hillside in fans, Southern California, 1953.

I don't think anybody knows what they have on screen. The good Lord has something to do with that. I enjoyed getting up and entertaining and the reaction you got from people, it was just, it was beautiful.

(opposite) Roy and Trigger on stage, entertaining at the Hollywood Canteen, 1942.
(below) Publicity still for RED RIVER VALLEY, 1941.

(opposite) "I spent most of the war entertaining troops."
(below) "Just posing for pictures was a job, let alone all the other stuff."

I appreciate the things those pictures did for me, but I just, I've got to believe there's somebody bigger than you and me, that there's a reason you're successful. You have some little thing, whatever it is, whether it's personality, some charisma that reaches the general public. I always felt a responsibility to the kids, to be somebody they could look up to.

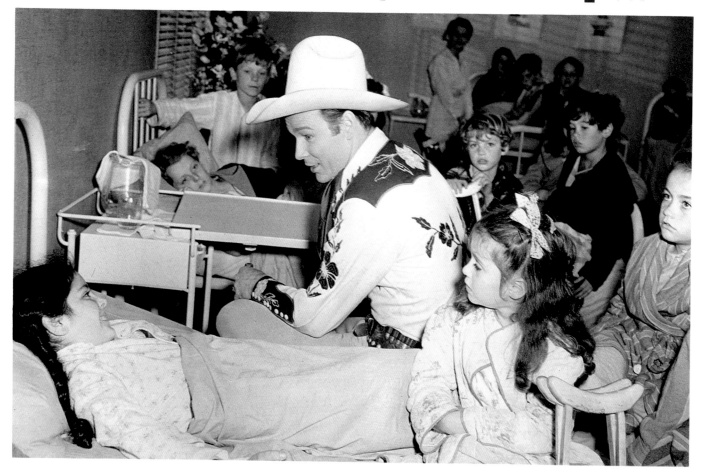

I feel like I've grown up with everybody that's alive today. I don't know, but there haven't been a lot of people as busy as I have been for so long and still alive! Ol' Roy Rogers. Course, my grandchildren and great-grandchildren when they were little, they had to have explained to 'em . . . "Who is that cowboy?"

(opposite) Roy and Jane Frazee in studio, shooting ON THE OLD SPANISH TRAIL, 1947.
(below) Publicity still for
THE RANGER AND THE LADY, 1940.

(above left) Len Slye on right with Duck Run school pals, about 1918. (above right) Roy and Dale with Roy's blind uncle Bill by the houseboat he helped build, Portsmouth, Ohio, 1956. (below left) Roy's mother's folks, (l to r), Farina, Possum, Blanche and Phineas Womack, Beefhide, KY, 1914. (below right)"Hair white as cotton," Little Len at 5, Union St. School, Portsmouth, Ohio, 1916. (opposite) Len (in white) with classmates at Duck Run School, Duck Run, Ohio, 1925.

My dad and his brother, my blind uncle Bill, built a houseboat when I was just a baby and they put us on it and we headed for Portsmouth on the Ohio River, from Cincinnati. They had somebody pulling and pushing them all along the river. I don't know how Mom did it with us babies, but we lived on that houseboat till I was 8 years old.

Uncle Bill stayed there on the boat till he died at 92. Within six months the houseboat was just disintegrated. Fans tore pieces off it. It just disappeared!

We lived on this houseboat till I was 7 or 8 and then we moved out to the countryside. Duck Run was 12 miles out of Portsmouth, Ohio, out on rough roads. In those days you just didn't travel the mud roads very often. I only saw a few movies, maybe a movie a year if I was lucky.

I had to learn farming, and

Roy age 12, with champion sow, Evangeline, who won him a trip to Columbus, Ohio, 1923.

experience is the best teacher. Now we had an old mule named Tom and I learned to plow with him. I was so little I had to reach up, to get a hold of the plow handles.

Dad worked in a shoe factory in Portsmouth and he'd only come home for a weekend

every 2 weeks. In the wintertime the ruts in the road would be a foot deep in the mud. So I never really got acquainted with my dad then. From 8 years old on, I missed him a lot. I was the only boy on the farm and I had to be the dad, kinda.

He didn't know anything about farming. In fact one of the mules kicked him and nearly crippled him. I was so mad I went back and stuck a pitchfork into that mule!

(above) Roy's dad, Andy Slye, clowning for the camera, 1940.
(below) "Dad taught me it never hurt to dream." Mattie and Andy Slye, 1939

When I was about 11 or 12 years old it seemed like just about all I did was gather eggs and shovel chicken droppings!

Mom and Dad played the mandolin and guitar and that's where we learned. We lived way back in the hills and that's where we had to entertain ourselves. At night we'd sit around,

mom, the girls and me, and we learned to play mandolin and guitar. That's how we got started, really. We learned to sing just to entertain ourselves. It was fun to sing, rather than just sit around and argue or something. The neighbors would come over and we'd have square dances. I called square dances by the time I was ten years old.

(Opposite, clockwise)
Len, Cleda, Kathleen and Mary
Slye, Portsmouth, Ohio, 1926.
(top left) The house Roy built
with his Dad when he was 11
years old, Duck Run, Ohio.
(top right) Roy, age 12,
Hanging Rock, Ohio.
(below) Roy on mandolin, his
mom on guitar, with his
family just after Roy and Dale's
wedding, January, 1948.

(above) Mattie Slye and her son.
(opposite, l to r) Mary, Kathleen,
Mattie, Len, Andy and Cleda Slye,
Lawndale, California, 1934.

Mom never did call me Roy. She says, "Honey, I just can't call you Roy." And I says, "Well, you call me Leonard," and she did. She called me Leonard right up to the end. I can understand it. I was her baby boy, you know? I had three lovely sisters and we just had a great family.

I always dreamed of being a doctor but I guess I was about 16 when I went to work in the shoe factory in Cincinnati with my dad. That was the beginning of the Depression. So we worked there for a couple of years. We got up one morning, my Dad and me in Cincinnati, and he says, "Son, let's quit our jobs and go to California." I says, "Well that's great. I saved up 90 bucks and that'll buy a lot of

(above) Len Slye with his brother-in-law Josie, Lawndale, California, 1930.
(opposite) The Slye family heads for California, with dog Ranger, Spring, 1930.

gas." We came to California in 1930. I read John Steinbeck's THE GRAPES OF WRATH and there are parts in that book that make me wonder if Mr. Steinbeck wasn't looking over the shoulders of the Slye family.

It was just impossible to find a job in those days, (the early 30's) so my sister talked me into trying out on an amateur radio show called Midnight Frolic. It was on every Saturday night from midnight 'til six in the morning and anybody could go on it.

Len (right) with cousin Stanley, summer, 1931. (opposite) Len in his first singing group, the Rocky Mountaineers, 1932.

I'll never forget, I was scared to death. I was about 18 at the time. When they announced my name I just froze to my seat and she came over and got me by the shoulders and says, "You get up there and sing," so I did. And to this day I couldn't tell you what songs I sang. I couldn't get out of there quick enough. So three days later I got a call from a guy who said he'd like me to join their group, the Rocky Mountaineers. And that's basically the start of my musical and entertaining career.

SHORTY LEFTY SLUMGUR

BB HI LEN BOB

"YOURS TRULY, ROCKY MOUNTAINEERS"
SORED BY WESTERN PAC. INVESTMENT

We had a barnstorming trip down through New Mexico, Arizona, Texas in 1933. And that was the hungriest trip anybody ever had. We ate jackrabbits and everything else on the road. In Roswell, New Mexico, we got

(opposite) Len (second from right) in a short-lived group, the International Cowboys, January, 1933. (above) Arlene Wilkins marries Len Slye. Roswell, N.M., July 3, 1936.

on a little radio station and we got to kidding one another on the air about what we'd like to eat. So I said lemon pie and that's how I met my first wife, Arlene. I got a phone call. If I would sing the Swiss Yodel they'd have a lemon pie for us. So we couldn't wait to get back to our little motel room. And here came this car and it had this pretty girl in it and her mother and two great big lemon pies. We couldn't wait for them to leave. . . couldn't eat fast enough. . . we just inhaled those things!

When I started the Sons of the Pioneers, we found a boarding house just two blocks away from KFWB at nine dollars a week. And that's 3 meals a day! So we holed up there and that's where the Sons of the Pioneers learned all these songs. It was a lot of hungry times in the early 30's, but fun.

(above) Farley's Gold Star Rangers, a forerunner of the Sons of the Pioneers, performing at KFWB Radio, Los Angeles, 1933.
(opposite) The Sons of the Pioneers in a publicity shot from Roy's film debut, THE OLD HOMESTEAD, Liberty Pictures, 1935. (clockwise) Bob Nolan, Hugh Farr, Tim Spencer, Karl Farr and Len Slye.

The Sons of the Pioneers did a lot of recordings and transcriptions and stuff and we became known as a singing group. When the music side of cowboy pictures started coming in, why, we were invited to come out to Republic Pictures and sing with Gene (Autry) and other different cowboys and the

Three Mesquiteers. At Columbia we sang with Charlie Starrett. And we were at a radio show over at KNX Hollywood, The Hollywood Barn Dance.

(left) Sheet music for Bob Nolan's, "Tumbling Tumbleweeds." (right) Sons of the Pioneers in a Republic picture, IDAHO, 1943.

Publicity shot for UNDER WESTERN STARS, 1938.

I was at the cleaners picking up my hat, cause I couldn't afford a new one, and a guy came in, he almost took the door off, all excited. He said, "I'm going out to Republic, they're looking for a new singing cowboy. I'm going out this afternoon for a screen test." So the next morning I saddled my guitar and went out there.

I didn't have an appointment. The guard on the gate wouldn't let me in, so I waited around 'til about noon when the extras started coming back from lunch and there was a big bunch of extras, so I just walked in with them. I just got inside the door when a hand fell on my shoulder and I thought it was a guard. I turned around and Sol Siegal, the producer of Western pictures, called me by my first name. I said "I heard you were looking for a new singing cowboy and I thought I'd take a chance." He says, "Well," he says, "That's why I stopped you. You never once entered my mind 'til you walked through that door!"

Republic arranged a screen test and I signed up there October 13th, 1937 and I made my first picture in January, 1938. I became Roy Rogers on my first picture.

(opposite) Roy and Smiley Burnette on location for UNDER WESTERN STARS, 1938.
(above) Publicity shot for UNDER WESTERN STARS, 1938.

(above) Roy's first starring western, UNDER WESTERN STARS premieres in Dallas, Texas, April, 1938.
(opposite inset) Roy Rogers saves the day in climactic chase scene, UNDER WESTERN STARS, 1938.

UNDER WESTERN STARS was my first Roy Rogers picture. It was the first B western that ever premiered on Broadway. I don't think I realized then, but the studio took me everyplace, nearly every state in the Union this whole first year, to openings and premieres of the picture. So I, uh, knew that the people liked it because of the reactions I got on my personal appearances.

When I first started at Republic Pictures, they liked what they saw in my screen test and when I made my first picture they wouldn't let me see the rushes. They were afraid if I saw myself on screen I'd try to improve on it and change it and they didn't want me to. They wanted me to play Roy Rogers, you know?

(above) Roy and Mary Hart, who also used the
name Lynn Roberts, in COME ON RANGERS, 1938.
(opposite) Republic publicity shot, 1938.

For my first picture they said, "You're gonna have to have a horse. You don't make cowboy pictures without a horse." So they called all the stables to send out the cast horses, the pretty horses. I was there the day they all came and I think  Trigger was about the third horse I got on and I never looked at the rest of them. Cause I knew, just from how he handled himself and how pretty, he was a gold color, I knew that they couldn't make any-thing any better than this one. Not only in action but in looks too. So that was it.

(opposite inset) Working with Trigger, 1949.
(opposite below) Roy and Trigger in
SON OF PALEFACE, with Bob Hope and Jane
Russell for Paramount, 1952.
(below) Roy and Trigger publicity
still that was often signed for fans,
"Many Happy Trails, Roy Rogers and Trigger"

Horses are like people. Everybody's got a different personality. Trigger had a  **different personality. He was a stallion, but you'd never know it, he was just so gentle and kind. And he had a great rein on him as a cowpony. I've had several of my kids on**

(above) Linda Lou and Cheryl Rogers keep the stallion under control, 1945.
(opposite) Publicity shots of the great horse, 1946-48.

him at one time, from his ears back to his tail and he would just. . . aw, he was a fabulous horse.

Trigger made every picture. He was 4 and I was 26 when we made our first picture. And Trigger lived to be 33. He was . . . he was something. I think it was 86 features plus 100 TV shows. Trigger made them all.

My double at one time was Joe Yrigoyen and they would try a stunt with two or three dou-

ble horses and they would all shy away from whatever they were supposed to do. So that's when Billy Witney (the director) would say "Bring up the old man." He'd always ask me if it was all right, cause I didn't want to hurt Trigger, y'know, like when they were rolling barrels downhill behind a truck. Fifty gallon drums. So we were coming behind it and Trigger'd have to jump those things. They came right at him and he jumped it. But it's a scary thing to watch because that was like my child out there doing those silly things.

"Trigger seemed to know when people were watching him. I think he knew the applause. He just ate it up, like a ham!"

I just tried to make them (the pictures) all as good as we possibly could. But the one I probably got the most kick out of was when I made the first one. The fact that I was starting out, still in the Depression years, it was new to me and it was a thrill to do it, you know?

(above and right) Roy Rogers, Hollywood, California, 1936. (opposite) Smiley Burnette, Roy and Carol Hughes in UNDER WESTERN STARS, 1938.

Coming out of the Depression and, golly I started out making 75 bucks a week and that's twice as much as I ever made . . . so I was as happy as a dead pig in the sunshine, you know?

I'd go on the road and come back after two or three months and make another picture and then go back on the road and it was just continuous. All the time.

Studios booked the little theaters for my tours. One tour I made, I played 135 shows in twenty days, I think it was. Five and six shows a day in these little theaters. They'd just fill 'em up, run a picture, I'd do a show, then they'd run a picture again, I'd do another show. Boy, I'll tell you, I really worked.

(Opposite) Exhausted cowboy on the road.
(below) Roy and Trigger wowing fans in front of the
Arcadia Theater, Temple, Texas, Feb. 16, 1943.

(four photos above) "Golly, I had such long days for years and years." Roy and Trigger on the road. Late '30's-1940's.
(far left) "Catching 40 winks" in the dressing room at Madison Square Garden, October, 1955.
(left) Roy's silver saddle arrives by armored car.
(opposite) A cowboy at home, packing for the road.

I entertained at hospitals and orphanages all the time. If I had Trigger with me, I'd generally take him. I had rubber boots I'd put on him, so he wouldn't slide on the slick hospital floors, leather with rubber soles. We'd buckle 'em on his legs and he'd go right up into the hospital rooms where the kids are. Take him up on elevators and everything. He was something.

(opposite above) Roy sings for the kids in the Children's Home, Allentown, PA.
(opposite below) Art and life mix in a scene from SONG OF TEXAS, 1943.
(above) "The little boys always wanted to see my guns, so I'd always show them my guns and sing a song or something."

They knew I was coming and sometimes they'd get the kids in a big room where I could entertain them and work Trigger at the same time. Probably some of them had never even seen a horse before. It was really nice. The little kids, some of 'em couldn't raise their hands but they'd have smiles all over their faces.

There's something romantic about winning the West, the history of it and the characters that came out. We had some historic pictures, like **BILLY THE KID RETURNS**, where Billy the Kid started the picture out and then I would show up and I looked like him and I'd play both parts. So I'd be accused of killing somebody. And **JESSE JAMES AT BAY** was another mistaken identity thing.

But I liked to do the modern pictures better. We did stories about what was going on at the time and I think that's why they were so popular, because people could relate to them.

(above) Roy as the good guy in JESSE JAMES AT BAY, 1941.
(opposite) In a modern story of intrigue around oil wells and railroad rights-of-way, Roy takes a bead on the bad guys Hal Taliaferro and John Carradine in SILVER SPURS, 1943.

I never considered myself an actor. I'd read a script and I'd just do it like I heard it, you know? If I was a bad guy I knew I wasn't supposed to smile and a good guy had a pleasant personality, so that's what I did. I was just natural.

(opposite) Roy in a rare dramatic role as Claire Trevor's hot-headed kid brother, with Walter Pidgeon and John Wayne in Republic's DARK COMMAND, 1940.
(below) Roy as the wounded hero in YOUNG BILL HICKOK, 1940.

I'd get up at 4, 4:30 in the morning and drive to the studio, make up, drive to location. You got the sun up in the morning and you'd chase the sun over the hill that evening and then you'd drive back to the studio and then you'd drive home. So it was a long day . . . part of it fighting and riding. You didn't have any trouble going to sleep, and you stayed in condition, I'll tell you that. I was in great physical shape in those days.

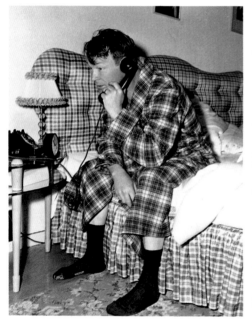

(left) The King of the Cowboys drags out of bed.
(above) "A daily dip keeps him at 165 lbs.— good riding weight." (Movie Life Yearbook, 1948).
(opposite) Roy mixes it up with William Haade, IN OLD CHEYENNE, 1941.

I always had squinty eyes, you know? The studio worried about me not having big bedroom eyes, so they sent a first aid man out on location with us and every so often he'd come by and drop these drops in my eyes so I could open them a little bit more. But it's funny, after my first picture came out, some of the first letters I got had some remarks that they liked the squinty eyes and the outdoor look

that I had. Several letters mentioned about the eyes, so the studio forgot about putting the stuff in my eyes after that.

(opposite) Publicity still for RED RIVER VALLEY, 1941.
(below) Under the glare of sunlight and reflectors, shooting UNDER WESTERN STARS, 1938.

The only thing that bothered me when the first picture came out, was that I started get-  **ting fan mail and I got, I mean literally thousands of letters. I had to hire 4 girls to answer the fan mail. I felt it was very important to answer the mail and I took it to Mr. Yates at Republic Pictures and he didn't want to have anything to do with it. I said, "Well, those people writing me are the ones paying 10 cents at the box office to see the pictures and I think it's very important." So I continued to do it.**

(opposite) One week's worth of fan mail, 1948.
(above) Trigger meets his competition on the
Republic Pictures lot, 1944.

Arlene and I didn't have any children. We were married 4 years and it didn't look like we were going to have any. I was always around kids and I just wanted a child very bad and I saw this little girl in an orphanage in Dallas when she was six weeks old. They had 42 little babies. I got to the seventh crib and this little head popped up and looked me right in the eye. Yes. That was Cheryl, my oldest daughter.

And then my wife got pregnant and we had Linda and Dusty. And then we lost Arlene a few days after Dusty's birth, with an embolism. It was just overnight, you know. In a few hours. Very shocking situation.

(opposite) Roy and Arlene, Roswell, N.M., 1938.
(above left) Roy and Arlene at the beach with friends, 1939.
(above right) Macho cowboy clowning with wife Arlene, Christmas, 1942.
(below left) Roy and his little cowgirl Cheryl, riding her daddy's saddle, 1940.
(below right) Mom and Dad with Cheryl after her baby sister Linda Lou's birth, 1943.

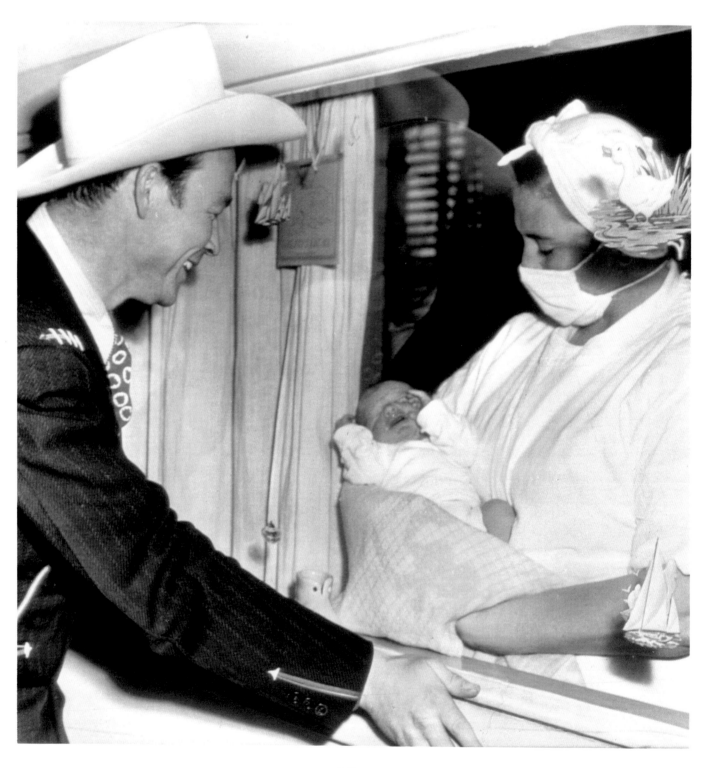

After Arlene's death I kept busy, kept my mind off it. At the time I'd played at hospitals all over the country, entertaining kids, crippled kids, people dying. I'd been around quite a bit. I had to accept it and I knew that. I was numb most of the time. I told the kids, "Mama's gone with God in heaven, she won't be back." You do the best you know how and just keep on going.

(opposite) Proud papa with newborn Roy Rogers, Jr. (Dusty), October 28, 1946.
(above) Roy's parents gather around their widowed son and grandchildren.
(right) Roy has his hands full with movie-stardom and single fatherhood.

(above) Roy, his kids and Republic crew gathered for Dusty's first birthday party, 1947.
(opposite) Roy with his television production crew, on location for THE ROY ROGERS SHOW, 1951.

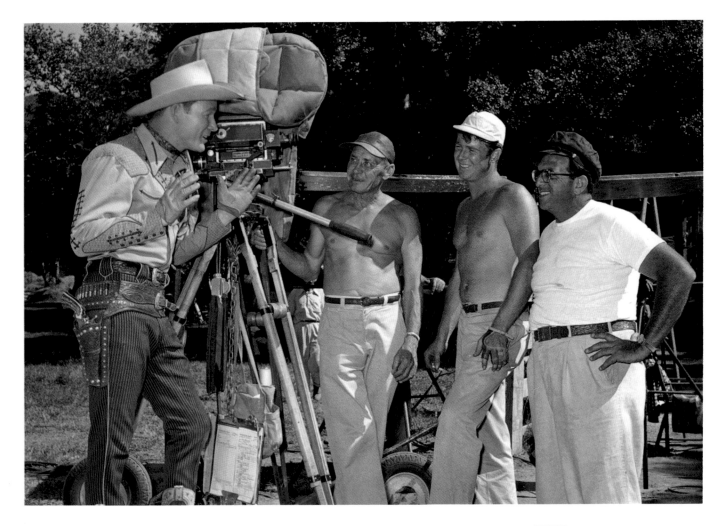

I was in love with all the crew. They were just terrific. And that's where my strength was, in the crew, 'cause they would try extra hard to get something good, rather than take it in one take and that was it. It was generally the cameramen and working people who were my friends.

Smiley Burnette was Gene's (Autry's) sidekick when he left the studio and so when they put me in the first picture he was still under contract. Smiley was fun to work with. I was fortunate to have some pretty good sidekicks, but Gabby, I have to say, I made more with Gabby than any of the rest of them.

(opposite) Roy and "Frog Millhouse"
(Smiley Burnette) in
HEART OF THE GOLDEN WEST, 1942.
(top left) Roy and "Teddy Bear"
(Guinn "Big Boy" Williams) in
HANDS ACROSS THE BORDER, 1944.
(top right) Roy and "Cookie Bullfincher"
(Andy Devine) in
BELLS OF SAN ANGELO, 1947.
(above left) Gordon Jones, Penny
Edwards and Roy in
TRAIL OF ROBIN HOOD, 1950.
(below right) Pat Brady (center) moved
on from sidekick role at Republic
to Roy's sidekick for the TV series.

I just loved old Gabby. He was a character. He was like my family. We did about forty, pictures together. He was like my father, my buddy and my brother all wrapped up in one. He wasn't anything like the character you see on the screen. He wore beautiful tweed suits and drove a Continental and he was straight as an arrow. But when he took his teeth out and put on that old suit, he became Gabby.

(below) Roy and "Gabby Whittaker" (George Hayes) in SUNSET SERENADE, 1942.
(opposite) George "Gabby" Hayes.

(opposite) Roy and Gabby in RIDIN' DOWN THE CANYON, 1942.
(opposite inset) "He was like my father, my buddy and my
brother all wrapped up in one. I can't say enough for him."
(below) Like all "dern, persnickety wimmin," Gale Storm
gets between Gabby and his man in RED RIVER VALLEY, 1941.

I got hit a couple of times in those fights and I hit a couple of guys in all those years. It's a little embarrassing when you hit somebody, especially a stuntman like Yakima Canutt. I pulled his neckerchief out and I couldn't see him, so I hit him right on the chin! I felt so awful. I picked him up and his teeth were chipped. I said, "Gosh, I'm sorry, Yak." You're hitting as hard as you can in these fights, but it's judging the distance. If the camera's in the right direction you can hit as hard as you can and the guy reacts to it as your fist crosses. I felt just awful.

(above) Roy flattens a bad guy in UNDER WESTERN STARS, 1938.
(opposite) "I give up..."

When we did running inserts we were flat out, 35-40 miles an hour, around there. I was very lucky I didn't get hurt during all those pictures. I've sprained a few ankles, things like that, but I never broke any bones. I'm real thankful I'm still here, because anything could happen, you know? Any kind of accident.

(opposite) Riding breakneck in
SHINE ON HARVEST MOON, 1938.
(above) "Of all the western stars,
I'd have to give Roy a perfect 10
in horsemanship." Bill Whitney,
director of 28 Roy Rogers films.

I appreciated the invitations to go to Hollywood parties, but I didn't know what to do after I got there. I just didn't speak most of their languages. The studio tried to get me to go to these parties because of the publicity, you know. And it really griped me. I'm just not a party person. I'd generally try to figure out some way I

(above) At ease with Clark Gable on the shooting range, 1959-1960.
(opposite above) "Roy Rogers helped Tommy Dorsey celebrate the 10th anniversary of his band at the Four Hundred Club." Tommy Dorsey, Frank Sinatra and Roy, around 1943-44.
(bottom left and right) Roy on the 1940's Hollywood party circuit.

could have somebody to talk to that I knew, so I'd take one of my hunting buddies with me, 'cause I'm basically a backward person.

I had some wonderful leading ladies down through the years and we had a chance to get acquainted making the pictures. That's a lot different than a Hollywood party where you've seen them on screen but you don't know them, don't know what makes them tick. It's kinda hard to carry on a conversation . . . always was for me.

(above left) Sally Payne (on right) played a cowboy's best friend, with Gale Storm in JESSE JAMES AT BAY, 1941.
(above) Roy and Jane Frazee in THE OLD SPANISH TRAIL, 1947.
(left) Penny Edwards and sidekick Gordon Jones teamed up with Roy in the1950-51 pictures.
(opposite, clockwise) Roy and Gale Storm in RED RIVER VALLEY, 1941. Roy torments a cocky Dale Evans in one of their 28 pictures together, SUNSET IN EL DORADO, 1945. Roy and Mary Hart (also known as Lynn Roberts) in SHINE ON HARVEST MOON, 1938. Lynn Carver and Beryl Wallace torment Gabby in SUNSET IN THE DESERT, 1942.

I could never see why, if a guy is going to like a girl in the picture, why they can't have them doing something, instead of standing around with a grin and looking pretty, you know? When Dale came along, she got into the fights and everything! She gave the leading lady a better part, and the people liked it! She could play the smart aleck newspaper gal and it just made the whole picture good.

(opposite) Roy, Dale Evans and Gabby Hayes in SUNSET IN EL DORADO, 1945.
(below) Dale gets into the act, with some help from Bullet, on THE ROY ROGERS SHOW.

When I went to work with Roy I thought I was just going to do one picture, **THE COWBOY AND THE SENORITA**. But the exhibitors liked it and so they said, "Don't break this team up!" Well, I didn't want to be part of a team. I didn't want to be typed as just a cowgirl. I mean, I sang in nightclubs and with dance bands and on the radio. I loved horses, but the only thing I ever rode were goats on my uncle's farm in Texas. So I didn't think I was right for a western. But the people liked it and I think the reason they like it was because I was sort of a foil for Roy. I was the smart aleck and he taught me better about the West. I was a real tenderfoot and I think the kids kind of got a kick out of that. The girls, though, the little girls didn't like me much, 'cause they liked Roy. So many of them said, "I'm gonna marry Roy Rogers when I grow up!" But I got fan mail from a lot of boys.   **Dale Evans**

Dale Evans in THE TRESPASSER, 1947. Republic removed her from Roy's pictures after they were married, but fans demanded her back and the team was reunited in 1949.

In the pictures I made, I wasn't even allowed to kiss the girl, 'cause the little boys would say, "Leave that mushy stuff out of our pictures!" But I ended up marrying my lovely leading lady and we've been married 45 years now, the best years of my life. I have a lot to be thankful for.

(opposite) Roy and Dale relaxing on a fishing trip, 1949.
(above) A smooch from Trigger, 1947.

I didn't say I wasn't kissing anybody, I said I couldn't kiss the leading lady!

Dale and I were good friends a long time. And I always respected Dale and always liked her as a person. I proposed to Dale on Trigger when I was getting ready to enter the stadium in Chicago. Then I rode off and I didn't get my answer till she rode out and nodded her head yes. We were married on New Year's Eve.

(opposite) A saucy duo file for their marriage license, December, 1947.
(above left) "They both looked like scared rabbits." (a wedding observer).
(above right) Roy and Dale are wed, New Year's Eve, 1947.

I think marriage is a give 80 and take 20 on both sides. And especially today, for marriages to survive, that's the way it's gotta be. You've got to give a lot more than you take, on both sides, and it's gotta be that way. Otherwise it's not a happy situation.

The King of the Cowboys and his Queen of the West. "I found him to be just as plain as an old shoe and comfortable, you know, and he was what he was. He didn't have any Hollywood facade. He was the same offscreen as he was in front of the camera and I respected that."

We have a wonderful family. Nine children altogether. We've had our share of tragedies too. We lost three of them. But you just keep on going. The press has been really good to me down through the years. But we have had a few bad ones. We had one reporter . . . to this

day, if I ever run across him I want to poke him right in the nose. He said the only reason Roy Rogers and Dale Evans were adopting children was for publicity! I could pinch his head off, I'm telling you! Even now, I would hit him. I don't know how far I could knock him today, but at 80 years old, well . . . I'll tell you, it hurt me. He's probably never been in an orphanage and seen little kids without moms and dads. And I had been in a lot of them. I've seen the other side, the sick side of 'em and the lonely side. And I tried to take up the space. We've had 4 adopted and 1 foster child. It's been a wonderful family life.

(above inset) Dale with son Tom Fox, Dusty in foreground, 1948.
(opposite) On tour, in Columbus, Ohio, August, 1956. (clockwise) Marion, Dale, Sandy, Dodie, Debbie, Dusty, Roy, Linda and Cheryl Rogers.

Robin was like a little delicate flower. We lost her two days before her second birthday. She had a very weak heart when she was born and she was a Downs Syndrome little girl. She was like a hothouse flower, you

know. She was so delicate.

But her little life and Dale's book, **ANGEL UNAWARE**, probably affected millions of people across the country. It still does. It helped a lot of people to bring their kids out of the back rooms. You know, I think it helped.

After we lost her, I took Dale to get out of town. We visited her mother in Texas and on the way home I asked her if she wanted to stop by Hope Cottage (orphanage) to see a little Indian baby she had told me about. She said, "I don't know if I could stand going there and seeing those babies." Well, when we got there, I was barely around the back of the car when Dale was inside with that little Indian baby in her arms. The officials said they had to place her with an Indian family and I said, "I have Choctaw blood in me." That's our daughter Dodie.

(opposite) Robin Elizabeth with her adoring parents, 1952.
(right) Dale and daughter Dodie, 1957.

On the same trip, I was playing a stadium in Cincinnati and I got a call from a lady who wanted to bring a little girl in a wheelchair to the show. She had a home for crippled kids in Covington, Kentucky. I said, "You wouldn't happen to have a little boy, 'cause

(above) Roy Jr. ("Dusty", right) meets his new brother, Harry John David ("Sandy"), autumn, 1952. Roy once said, "If I had another boy I guess I'd have to name him 'Filthy'." (opposite inset) Cheryl and Linda meet their new baby sister Mary Little Doe, ("Dodie"), while Dusty looks on.

my son Dusty is kinda tired being around all the girls. "She said, "Well, I have one, but you probably wouldn't be interested in him." I said, "Can you bring him tonight?" So when Dale and I came offstage after the first act, here stood little Sandy in a yellow corduroy suit and a short cap and he stuck

his little hand out and said, "Howdy pardner!" Well, we both died right there. So we got Sandy and then stopped off in Dallas to pick up Dodie and we got home with two of them on the same trip.

All the kids met us at the airport and you should have seen the faces! Dusty, I can see him standing back, looking at Sandy, now, after he'd already asked for a brother, you know? But after he'd seen him, he didn't know whether it was a good idea.

I thought a good way for them to get acquainted was to go out and rough it on a camping trip, the three of us together. So we took off in the car and we were gone for 2 weeks. We did our own cooking and caught fish and frogs and rabbits and we'd cook 'em. We had a sleeping bag that the two of 'em crawled in together. And when we came back home from that trip, they were really brothers. They just loved one another from then on.

Debbie, bless her heart, she was something. This friend of ours was a minister in Korea during the war. He picked a lot of kids up off the street who were half-Korean, from the soldiers, and put an orphanage together. We asked him for a little girl Dodie's age. One that looked a lot like her, 'cause the kids in school would kid Dodie, who wasn't their same color. Debbie's mother was Korean

(opposite) Dusty and Sandy soon become inseparable on a camping trip with Dad.
(above) Ai Lee ("Debbie") and Dodie ride their favorite bronco.

and her father was Puerto Rican. So they grew up together and looked like sisters.

At one time we had 400 articles on the market with my name on it. Gun holsters and all that stuff. We had a lot of little outfits for the kids. Sold by the jillion!

(above) Roy's own Comic Book series with Dell Publishing Co. hit the news stands January, 1948. The cowgirl is reading comic #43, issued July, 1951.
(opposite) The Roy Rogers Corral offered merchandise displayed for department stores. In 1953, the Roy Rogers Plus Brand reported sales of 408,000 pairs of felt RR slippers, 900,000 RR lunch kits, and 1,203,000 RR jeans and jackets.

It all started in 1945, '46. We were second to Walt Disney in commercial tie-ups. We made a lot of money at it, but I didn't get to save a lot of it. I was in the tax bracket that was just insulting to anybody . . . 91% to Uncle Sam! I never had any money all my life and all of a sudden to make a lot of money and have to give it all away. . . goes against my grain a little.

The time came when all the studios were fighting television and they thought they could whip TV. After my second contract was up, they called me in and wanted me to sign another seven years and I said "Only if I could have some television privileges," because at that time old pictures were starting to run on TV. And the minute I mentioned television, my boss went right through the roof. That's when I left and started my own series.

Pat Brady, Roy Rogers and Dale Evans were partners in adventure on THE ROY ROGERS SHOW.

The TV series was our own production. We made most of the shows on our ranch up at Chatsworth, cause we had big rocks and hills and we put in a little lake. We had 138 acres. We kept the horses right there. We had the running insert roads, the whole thing. We'd get up and get out of bed, get

into make-up, go out and start shooting right out the bedroom window. . . even used the house for some scenes.

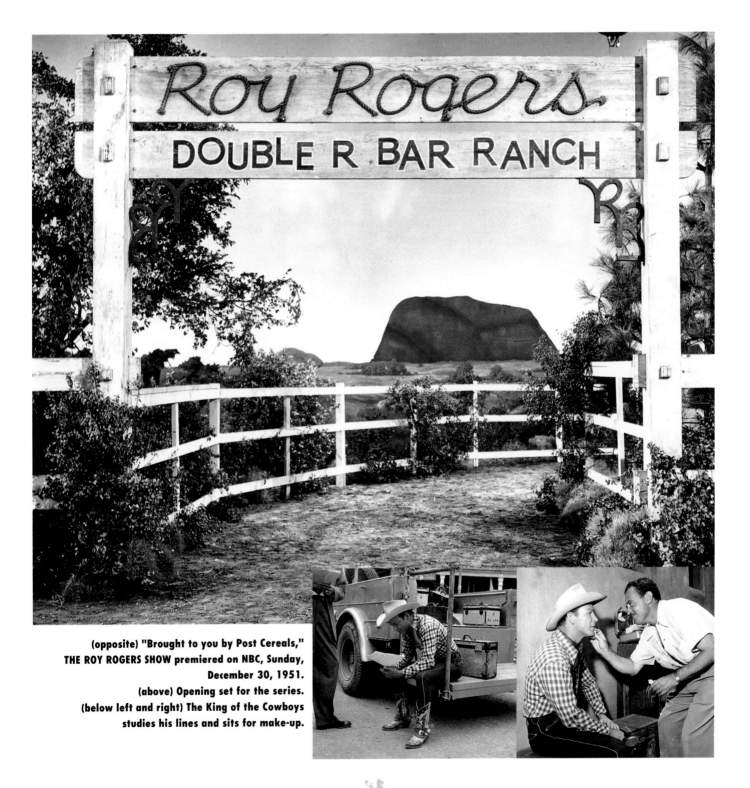

(opposite) "Brought to you by Post Cereals,"
THE ROY ROGERS SHOW premiered on NBC, Sunday,
December 30, 1951.
(above) Opening set for the series.
(below left and right) The King of the Cowboys
studies his lines and sits for make-up.

Harry Harvey played the old sheriff. And Pat Brady played the comedy part. I got him to do some things that were just ad-lib, you know? He had a rubber face. He could do anything with that face.

Right after World War II, the Jeeps were real popular. I always had one for hunting, going up steep hills and I'd drive to the studio in the morning and pass kids waiting for

(opposite) Dale ran the Eureka Cafe in Mineral City while Roy, Bullet, sidekick Pat Brady and, of course, Trigger, kept the peace in Paradise Valley.
(opposite inset) Harry Harvey played the Sheriff.
(above) Nellybelle was Pat Brady's "mount" for the show.

the bus and you could see them pointing to the Jeep, punching each other, saying there goes one, you know? So I thought if kids love Jeeps so much I'd put Pat Brady in the Jeep instead of a horse and that's how Pat got Nellybelle.

Dale's Buttermilk was a little quarter horse and he could turn so easy. I used to kid her all the time. She'd bounce and hit the saddle, but when we finished our TV shows, she could ride with anybody. She was real good at it!

(below) When Dale refused a double for the racing scenes in MY PAL TRIGGER, 1946, she got into trouble with the studio boss. (opposite) Dale on Buttermilk on THE ROY ROGERS SHOW, 1955.

Of course, I enjoyed making pictures, but it was a job. That's what it meant to me. The best part of my life is my family. And we had our share of hard times just like everybody else.

We lost our Debbie just before she was 12. She went on a church bus trip to an orphanage in Tijuana. Dodie was supposed to go too, but she had a cold. So Debbie loved to pass out clothing and stuff to the kids because she was an orphan too, and on the way home there was a head-on accident, and Debbie and her little friend and six other people were killed. It really turned our lives upside down for a while, till we got a hold of ourselves.

And then we lost Sandy in the service, you know. He always wanted to be a soldier. We lost three of our kids. We're just like all families. We had our share of tragedies along with all the good things.

Sandy and Debbie roughhouse with their Dad.

When I rode out in front of 105,000 people at the Coliseum, somebody asked me, "Isn't it frightening?" I said, "Naw, I was too dumb to get scared!"

Yeah, I was always nervous, I never did a show that I wasn't nervous. I'd be walking, pacing backstage, trying to think of what I was going to say. Dale's good at it, but I get nervous and jerky and I sometimes can't think of what I want to talk about, you know, I get excited. But you just go out there and be as natural as you can, like you're talking to Joe Doaks.

I did so many parades. And it could get dangerous, kids chasing after the cars, trying to get an autograph. You just can't sign one for one kid, 'cause then they'd pour into the street. That's why I was in better shape if I was riding Trigger, cause I had my hands full. Sometimes it was bedlam. It happened so many places.

(opposite) Roy and Trigger at the Sheriff's Rodeo, Los Angeles Coliseum.
(below) The press of the crowds.

(opposite) On tour in Hawaii, August, 1953.
(above) Roy and Trigger visit New York's Bellevue Hospital patients, October, 1955.

Old Nudie used to make our Western outfits, all those real fancy clothes we wore, the fringe and embroidery and stuff. He came out here from New York and I helped put him into business. He told me what he had in mind and it sounded good to me. We became good friends.

We used those clothes to great advantage. Kids loved the fancy stuff. Cowboys can get as dirty as they want to when they're working, but when it comes time for rodeo dress up, well you sparkle it up a little. We wore rhinestones, and when they'd black out the lights and hit you, you'd come alive.

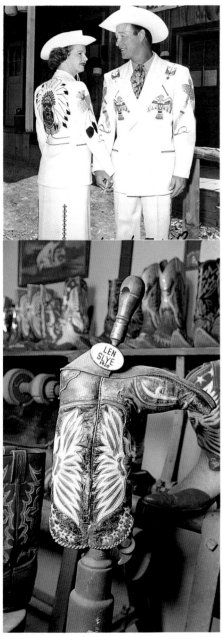

(opposite) A bit of Roy's wardrobe at the Roy Rogers and Dale Evans Museum, Victorville, California.
(above) Roy and Dale duded up, 1953.
(left) An old pair of Roy's boots on display at the museum.

(opposite) Roy puts his boot-print in cement at Graumann's Chinese Theater, April 21, 1949. (below) "I think of all I've been through and it's a wonder I'm still alive!" Roy, 1992.

(below) Roy, Bob Hope and Jane Russell in SON OF PALEFACE,
a comedy for Paramount, 1952.
(opposite) Roy in his last picture, MACKINTOSH AND T.J., 1975.

We don't ride anymore, no. We're both a little too old for that kind of stuff. You bruise yourself a little bit and it hurts for a week, you know what I mean? So we just don't push ourselves. Course I do ride the motorcycle. If I had Trigger I'd still be riding.

I put those guns on the other day and I thought I had a forty pound load on me. It just felt ten times heavier than it used to. I'd do running mounts and everything with them on. I don't think I could get off the ground with them now!

(opposite) Roy performs a "running dismount" from Trigger in NIGHT TIME IN NEVADA, 1948.
(below) Roy and Dale riding Trigger in LIGHTS OF OLD SANTA FE, 1944.

They threw away the pattern when they made Trigger. He was the greatest horse, without a doubt, that ever came along. If there's a heaven for horses, that's where he is. Old Trigger was 33 when he died and I just couldn't bury him. After seeing how they mount animals in the Smithsonian, I had Trigger mounted rearing on his hind legs. I put a brand new silver saddle on him and I like to tell Dale, "When I pass away just skin me and put me up on Trigger and I'll be happy!"

(above) Roy Rogers at 76, 1987.
(opposite) Roy and Trigger's signature rearing shot, from their first film together, UNDER WESTERN STARS, 1938.

I feel like I've kind of touched the lives of a lot of wonderful people and they've certainly been nice to me.

Roy and Trigger pleasing the fans at the Hollywood Christmas Parade, 1950.

(top left) Roy and Dusty fight the comic book bad guys.
(top right) Mayor Fiorello LaGuardia welcomes Roy and Trigger to New York, 1955.
(bottom left) Roy enjoying his female fans.
(bottom right) Sandy Rogers, 1950.

ACKNOWLEDGMENTS

Jim Bowman	Nancy Pollard
Jim Cornfield	Paul Pollard
Dale Evans	Mondo & Mary Lou Polverari
Don Jim	Roy Rogers, Jr.
Petra Lent	Roy Rogers and Dale Evans Museum
Lawson Little	Ira Schreck
Jack Mathis	Jane & Herbert Searle
Len Morris	Green and Tillisch Photography
Stan Moress	Jim & Judy Wilson
Robert Phillips	Suzie Zost